HEALTH

JUMP START
30-Day
MEAL
PLANNER

VALERIE
SAXION, N.D.

Strength & Honor

BRONZE BOW PUBLISHING
MINNEAPOLIS, MINNESOTA

JUMP START 30-DAY MEAL PLANNER

I am excited that you have a copy of *The Gospel of Health*, and my prayer is that God will use it to provide you with the insight you need to walk in the fullness of health. I firmly believe that vibrant health through natural treatments is God's will for your life.

The key to health begins with the nutrients you take into your body. My intent in this planner is to guide you into some simple, inexpensive, healthy meals that will boost your brainpower and fuel your energy levels. Through the wise choices you make, you can reshape your diet to be the best it can be.

Many of the meals are ones that our family enjoys on a daily basis. If you are interested in specific recipes for some of the entrées in this planner, you can find them in my book, *Super Foods for Super Kids*. Don't let the title fool you. These recipes are kid friendly, but they're for everyone else as well!

Many blessings,

Valerie Saxion, N.D.

DAY 1

BREAKFAST
Avocado Swiss omelet
Salsa for topping
1/2 grapefruit
1 piece Ezekiel bread

LUNCH
All-beef kosher meat dog on whole grain bun
Crunchy nut granola
Cinnamon applesauce
Lemon ginger tea

DINNER
Turkey breast
Mixed green salad
Sweet potato

HEALTHY CHOICE

AVOCADOS are unique among the fruits in that they are a very concentrated food, more like a nut than a fruit. They are high in calories—one average avocado has about 300 calories and about 30 grams of fat, as well as 12 grams of carbohydrate and 4 to 5 grams of protein. They are a good source of fat for people who have a problem assimilating other fatty  foods. They are fairly high in most of the B vitamins except B12, being particularly good in folic acid, niacin, and pantothenic acid. They also have some vitamin C, good amounts of vitamin A, and contain a bit of vitamin E. Avocados are very rich in potassium and are also particularly good in many other minerals, including magnesium, iron, and manganese. Avocados are commonly used in salads, dips such as guacamole, in sandwiches, or stuffed with seafood.

DAY 2

BREAKFAST
Chocolate/almond butter/banana smoothie

LUNCH
Almond butter and banana on Ezekiel bread
Salad
Carrot sticks
Red Zinger tea

DINNER
Lamb roast
Red potatoes
Green beans
Salad

HEALTHY CHOICE

ALMOND BUTTER is made from raw almonds. Almonds are probably the best all-around nut. Their fat content is less than most, about 60 percent, and the protein concentration is nearly 20 percent. They are one of the richest sources of alpha-tocopherol vitamin E. The almond has strong medicinal action including inhibition of cancer. The almond nuts are the fruits of a small tree that grows nearly thirty feet tall and is abundant in many areas of the world, including Asia, the Mediterranean, and North America. Almonds which are of the soft-shell variety possess a sweeter nut than those in hard shells.

DAY 3

BREAKFAST
2 boiled eggs
1/2 avocado sliced with healthy ranch dressing drizzled on top
Fresh mango slices

LUNCH
Preservative-free turkey breasts sliced medium thin with provolone cheese, cream cheese, sliced and cubed cucumber, and flaxseeds rolled into tight cylinders.
All natural Cheetos®
Fresh strawberries
Granola bar
Orange Zinger tea

DINNER
Salmon
Rice pilaf
Asparagus
Salad

HEALTHY CHOICE

FLAXSEEDS are the richest source there is for the Omega-3 fatty acids. They contain up to 40 percent oil, primarily linoleic and linoleic acids, which are excellent for strengthening the immune system, alleviating rheumatoid arthritis, clearing the heart and arteries, and helping prevent cancer. It has antibacterial, antifungal, and antiviral properties and can be ground and used as a raw condiment or supplement.

DAY 4

BREAKFAST
Creation's Bounty smoothie

LUNCH
High protein fruit salad with chopped pecans
Barbecue chicken wings or legs
Apple wedges with almond butter
Lemonade

DINNER
Grilled chicken salad
Rice crackers

HEALTHY CHOICE

PECANS are a relative of walnuts and a
member of the hickory genus. They
are low in sodium and high in most
other minerals, including zinc,
iron, phosphorus, potassium,
selenium, and magnesium.
Copper, calcium, and manganese
are also present in good amounts.
Pecans contain some vitamins A, E, and C,
niacin, and other B vitamins. Of all the nuts, pecans are second
only to macadamias in fat (over 70 percent) and contain the
lowest protein (about 10 percent). Shells should be light
brown.

DAY 5

BREAKFAST
2 eggs fried in olive oil
Fakin' bacon
Fresh orange slices
1/2 low-carb English muffin

LUNCH
Fruity pasta salad with raisins, mandarin oranges, and walnuts
Barbecue chicken wings or legs
Apple wedges with almond butter
Lemonade

DINNER
Roasted chicken
Stir fry veggies
Brown rice

HEALTHY CHOICE

RAISINS are full of iron, potassium, magnesium, phosphorus, and calcium, as well as vitamins A and B-complex. If you take 1 pound of grapes and dehydrate them, you'll have .25 pound of raisins. Raisins are still sun-cured, which enhances their flavor. Unfortunately, raisins contain the highest levels of pesticide residue of any fruit, so buy organic raisins. To keep raisins from becoming dry when baking, plump them in water for 15 minutes before mixing into baked goods.

DAY 6

BREAKFAST
Salmon
Organic cream cheese
Low-carb bagel
Fresh papaya

LUNCH
Chicken salad
Pita bread
Carrot sticks
Dill pickles
Red Zinger tea

DINNER
Black beans/yellow rice
Salad

HEALTHY CHOICE

CHICKEN BREAST is a wonderfully lean meat that I use all the time. A portion size of 1/2 breast delivers 26 protein grams and only 3 fat grams in contrast to a 3-ounce portion of red meat that brings 23 protein grams and 13 fat grams. The fattiest parts of a chicken are the wings, which have a lot of skin and little meat, and the thighs. Always remove the skin to cut out the fat.

DAY 7

BREAKFAST
Spinach feta omelet
Turkey sausage
1 slice of Ezekiel bread

LUNCH
Salmon salad with sunflower seeds, avocado, and mandarin oranges
Ranch dressing
Barbara's Bakery lemon yogurt granola bar
Red delicious apple
Lemon Zinger tea

DINNER
Roasted chicken
Couscous
Stir fry veggies

HEALTHY CHOICE

SUNFLOWER SEEDS contain complete proteins with only 20 percent fat, which is mostly unsaturated. As a complete protein, their nutritional value is complete without further preparation. They are a good source of zinc, calcium, phosphorus, and iron, as well as vitamins A, D, E, and several of the B-complex. Whole seeds have a good shelf life, but once hulled they should be refrigerated.

DAY 8

BREAKFAST
Oatmeal
Raisins
Almond slices
Fresh berries
1 slice of Ezekiel bread

LUNCH
Turkey salad with red onions
Whole grain bread or rice cakes or in pita bread
Granny Smith apple
Pretzel sticks
Oatmeal raisin cookie
Bottled water

DINNER
Mixed green salad
Organic soup
1 slice of rye toast

HEALTHY CHOICE

RED ONIONS contain the same potent antioxidant quercitin as other onions, but are a more concentrated source of it. The quercitin, along with the sulphur amino acids also in onions, helps to excrete toxic heavy-metal compounds that build up in the body. Onions also have  antibiotic, antiviral, and anti-candida properties. They contain sulfur compounds that lower cholesterol. When eaten regularly, onions are powerful fighters in the war on cancer and heart disease. They are 90 percent water and low in calories.

DAY 9

BREAKFAST
1 cup yogurt
1 cup fresh fruit
1/2 cup granola

LUNCH
Egg salad in a pocket with alfalfa sprouts and sunflower seeds
Granola bar
Snack bag of grapes
Concord grape juice

DINNER
Vanilla protein powder smoothie
Mixed green salad with salmon flakes on top

HEALTHY CHOICE

ALFALFA SPROUTS are up to 30 percent protein by dry weight and are an excellent source of chlorophyll, bioflavonoids, and carotenes. It acts as a laxative, improves the flow of urine, and is rich in nutrients. Almost as good as seaweed as a mineral source, alfalfa contains iron, sulfur, silicon, chlorine, cobalt,  magnesium, calcium, potassium, and zinc. It is by far the most common sprout to be in salads or sandwiches. They are very tasty but should be eaten fresh so that they do not ferment.

DAY 10

BREAKFAST
1/2 cup cottage cheese
1/2 cup fresh pineapple
1 boiled egg

LUNCH
Mashed sweet potatoes
Baby spinach salad
Sliced turkey breast
Cranberry juice

DINNER
Tuna steak
Brown rice
Steamed veggies
Mixed green salad

HEALTHY CHOICE

SWEET POTATOES are a wonderful source of vitamin E and also contain carotenoids, which are excellent antioxidants. A 5" x 2" baked sweet potato contains more than 2.5 times the U.S. Recommended Dietary Allowance and nearly 30 milligrams of vitamin C, or about a third of what you need in a day. That sweet potato also contributes 3.5 grams of fiber to your diet, all for just 117 calories.

DAY 11

BREAKFAST
2 poached eggs
Turkey sausage
Orange wedges
1 small whole grain muffin

LUNCH
Brown rice pilaf
Chicken fingers with honey
Mandarin oranges
Barbara's Bakery granola bar
Orange Zinger tea

DINNER
Salmon quesadillas
Salsa
Spinach salad

HEALTHY CHOICE

EGGS are nearly a perfect food. The protein is complete, with all the essential amino acids, and the ratio of minerals is perfect for the purpose of growth. They contain high amounts of vitamins A, D, and E as well as some B-vitamins. Because egg yolks contain fat and cholesterol, many people think they should avoid them, but cholesterol is required by the body to make hormones, including the stress-fighting steroid hormones. Also, they contain rich amounts of lecithin, which prevents cholesterol from working much of its trouble in the arteries.

DAY 12

BREAKFAST
1 medium sweet potato baked the night before, sliced in half, sautéed in olive oil until crisp on the outside and warm on the inside.

LUNCH
Lentil soup
Brown rice salad with dried cranberries and nuts
Celery stuffed with almond butter
Corn muffins
Lemonade

DINNER
Turkey salad
Organic soup
Iced green tea

HEALTHY CHOICE

LENTILS date back to the account in Genesis of 25:34 where Esau sold his birthright to Jacob for a tasty bowl of lentil stew. For centuries it has remained a dietary staple across Europe and the Middle East. It ranks just under soy as a top legume protein source, is mild to the taste, and benefits the heart and circulatory systems. They are high in calcium, magnesium, potassium, phosphorus, chlorine, and vitamin A.

DAY 13

BREAKFAST
Vanilla bean and berry smoothie

LUNCH
Vegetarian chili
1 slice of Ezekiel bread
Green salad topped with sunflower seeds, avocado chunks, and almond slivers
Fresh berries
Bottled water

DINNER
Stuffed baked potato
Fakin' bacon
Steamed broccoli
Cheddar cheese
Sea salt
Green salad

HEALTHY CHOICE

CHILI PEPPERS are a great source of vitamin C and other antioxidant nutrients, including beta-carotene. They have been used widely as natural remedies for coughs, colds, sinusitis, and bronchitis. There is some evidence that chilies help low-density lipoprotein (LDL), or bad cholesterol, and they raise your endorphin level, so you feel better.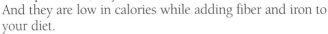
And they are low in calories while adding fiber and iron to your diet.

DAY 14

BREAKFAST
Veggie wrap

LUNCH
Black bean roll-ups
Blue corn chips
Orange wedges
Hibiscus tea

DINNER
Frozen organic veggie lasagna
Green salad

HEALTHY CHOICE

BLACK BEANS, or turtle beans, are members of the kidney bean family and are loaded with proteins. This is excellent protein with none of the hormones, pesticides, antibiotics, and other toxin residues that end up in animal protein. Black beans are sweet and spicy and taste great in soups or refried.

DAY 15

BREAKFAST
Yogurt parfait

LUNCH
Chicken burritos with chopped garlic cloves
Nutritious corn chips
Snack bag of almonds and raisins
Snack bag of orange slices
Ginseng cola

DINNER
Baked organic beef patty
Baked red potatoes
Salad

HEALTHY CHOICE

GARLIC has strong antimicrobial power and is more effective against pathogens than most antibiotics today. It is an excellent antioxidant that stimulates the number of immune cells and is antiviral and antiparasitic. Garlic is also a powerful force in reducing cholesterol and triglycerides and promotes the growth of healthy intestinal flora that are a key to health. It contains a compound called S-allylcysteine, which many experts believe contains the vegetable's anticancer agent.

DAY 16

BREAKFAST
Cappuccino smoothie

LUNCH
Barbecue tofu sandwich
Coleslaw
Baked beans
Oatmeal cookie with raisins and walnuts
Orange Zinger tea

DINNER
Lentil soup
Brown rice
Green salad

HEALTHY CHOICE

TOFU is the best known soy food in America and contains a full spectrum of naturally occurring soy isoflavones. It is made of soymilk curdled with nigari or calcium sulfate and takes on the consistency of a firm custard. It is an excellent food for heart health and cancer prevention. Combine it with the whole grain bun and you get an easily digested high-quality protein that is cholesterol-free and low in saturated fats.

DAY 17

BREAKFAST
Chicken strips sautéed in olive oil with veggies
Brown rice

LUNCH
Turkey burger
Carrot sticks
Dill pickles
Condiments
Applesauce

DINNER
Amy's frozen organic burrito
Veggie sticks
Chips and salsa

HEALTHY CHOICE

TURKEY is very low in fat, reasonably priced, and may be found in the natural and antibiotic-free state. It contains tryptophan, the essential amino acid that is the building block of serotonin and regulates our metabolism and induces sleep. A 3-ounce portion of turkey delivers 25 grams of protein and only 2 grams of fat.

DAY 18

BREAKFAST
12 ounces carrot/beet juice
2 boiled eggs
1 whole-grain crumpet or English muffin

LUNCH
Veggie burger with Swiss cheese
Dill pickle
Carrot sticks
Apple juice

DINNER
Chicken kabobs baked or broiled with favorite vegetable
Salad

HEALTHY CHOICE

SWISS CHEESE is a fantastic source of calcium, delivering 530 mgs. of calcium for every 2-ounce portion. Our need for calcium is critical during the growth years of infancy and childhood, for building healthy bones and teeth, but is also important lifelong to keep our bones healthy.

DAY 19

BREAKFAST
Pita bread
Hummus
Lamb
Fruit plate

LUNCH
Veggie stir fry
Cold salmon patties
Fresh cherries
Cheese straws
Lemon ginger tea

DINNER
6 baked chicken wings with organic barbecue sauce
Veggie plate with dip
Sautéed veggies

HEALTHY CHOICE

BANANAS are high in potassium, so they are good for keeping potassium levels up during periods of stress. Bananas are almost completely made up of carbohydrate. They contain many vitamins and minerals, including iron, selenium, and magnesium. Ripe bananas are good for digestive health and can help with constipation and diarrhea. Bananas are used in flavoring for desserts and banana bread, in breakfast cereals, or even in sandwiches. Most commonly, though, they are eaten after peeling the skin as a snack or dessert carried to work or school. As far as treats go, bananas are one of the healthiest, low-calorie snacks.

DAY 20

BREAKFAST
Salmon
Boiled egg
Avocado slices
Mango

LUNCH
Spinach quiche
Melon wedges
Crunchy granola w/carob chips, which is good by itself or on top of yogurt
Lemonade

DINNER
Veggie omelet with goat cheese
1 slice Ezekiel bread
Green salad

HEALTHY CHOICE

SPINACH contains calcium, folic acid, magnesium, potassium, riboflavin (vitamin B2), and vitamins C and K. Spinach also contains lutein, which has been linked to lowering levels of artery-  clogging fat deposits. Add in spinach, kale, collard greens, and other dark leafy green vegetables to your diet—use a few leaves of spinach instead of iceberg lettuce for sandwiches, for example, or chop up spinach leaves and add them to spaghetti sauce. Lightly cooked spinach is a delicacy, and it can be eaten raw as a salad green.

DAY 21

BREAKFAST
Open-face guacamole spread on Ezekiel bread toast with vine-ripened tomatoes
Tropical fruit smoothie

LUNCH
Barbecue chicken legs
Banana flan pie
Carrot salad
Yogurt pretzels and yogurt almonds
Bottled water

DINNER
2 slices organic pizza
Salad

HEALTHY CHOICE

TOMATOES are one of the most versatile food ingredients and a staple of the Mediterranean diet. They contain lycopene, a powerful pigment and antioxidant important in the prevention of cancer, as well as significant levels of vitamin E, less of vitamin C, and a small amount of beta-carotene. Tomatoes are a good source of the flavonoid substance quercetin. Canned tomatoes have similar nutritional values, except for lower carotenes and vitamin C. Dried tomatoes and tomato paste are excellent. Look out for the added salt in tomato juice.

DAY 22

BREAKFAST
1/2 cup granola
Raisins
Almonds
Sunflower seeds
Organic milk

LUNCH
Spaghetti pie
Diced apple and banana with 2 tablespoons of strawberry yogurt
Passion fruit dessert
Carrot sticks
Sparkling water with lime wedge

DINNER
Grilled or baked halibut
1/2 cup brown rice
Green salad
Brussels sprouts

HEALTHY CHOICE

CARROTS are rich in carotenes and an excellent source of chromium and fiber. Beta-carotene may help prevent cancer of the lungs, cervix, and gastrointestinal tract. Carrots also give your immunity system a boost. A 7"- to 8.5"-long carrot has more than 2,000 mg. of vitamin A—more than twice what you need in a day—and just 30 calories. You also get about 2 grams of fiber and nearly 250 milligrams of potassium. By the way, peeled baby carrots are not really babies. They are adult carrots whittled down.

DAY 23

BREAKFAST
Strawberry kefir
Ezekiel bread
1 boiled egg

LUNCH
Mediterranean flat bread pizza
Pineapple sticks
Cucumber rings with ranch dressing
Club soda with cranberry juice (half-and-half mixture)

DINNER
Trout almondine
Rice pilaf
Salad

HEALTHY CHOICE

MEDITERRANEAN FLAT BREAD is exactly what it says, flat bread. It does not rise like other bread because it does not have all the yeast. Much like tortillas or pita bread without the pocket, Mediterranean flat bread is wonderful for making wraps. Flat breads are carried in most stores and can be found with all natural organic whole wheat and a variety of other ingredients, including no yeast or salt.

DAY 24

BREAKFAST
Smooth Moves smoothie—prune juice, blackstrap molasses, organic rice milk, plain yogurt, organic banana, Creation's Bounty, and oat bran

LUNCH
Chicken cashew croquettes
Red grapes
All natural chips
Mango tea

DINNER
Pita pocket stuffed with chicken breast, greens, and small amount of dressing

HEALTHY CHOICE

CASHEWS are rich in magnesium, potassium, iron, selenium, and zinc. Calcium is lower in cashews than in other nuts, as is manganese; cashews also have a lower fat (47 percent) and higher carbohydrate level than most other nuts. They contain 20 percent protein. Some B vitamins are present, as is vitamin A, though very little vitamin E is found in cashews.

DAY 25

BREAKFAST
Pink zinger smoothie—freckled bananas, fresh strawberries, and pink grapefruit juice
Tuna packed in water

LUNCH
Salmon patties with extra virgin olive oil
Avocado wedges (nice to dip in ranch dressing)
Banana, apple yogurt salad
Carob chip and walnut cookie
Lemonade

DINNER
Amy's Lentil Loaf
Real mashed potatoes
Fresh or frozen green beans
Salad

HEALTHY CHOICE

EXTRA VIRGIN OLIVE OIL is by far the best oil you can use. It has been proven to be the healthiest for your heart as well as lowering your cholesterol level instead of clogging your arteries the way the saturated fats found in your typical grocery store oils and margarinated butter do. Stay away from Canola oil as well. Olive oil is far more versatile and can be used for just about anything.

Medicinally speaking, olive oil has proven to be a natural antibiotic as well as antiviral. It tastes great and is good for you!

DAY 26

BREAKFAST
1/2 cantaloupe
1 cup mixed strawberries, blueberries, and raspberries

LUNCH
Veggie burgers
Carrot, raisin, and pineapple salad
Dill pickles
Apple juice

DINNER
Sweet couscous
Sautéed chicken and veggie strips
Salad

HEALTHY CHOICE

COUSCOUS is a delicious variety of cracked wheat, smaller than the bulgur. It is also used commonly in the Middle Eastern diet—mutton and couscous is the traditional faire in those countries. Couscous is also very good with lentils or chickpeas, and this versatile grain can be used in a main dish, as a salad, or even in desserts. It is easily prepared by pouring boiling water over this soft grain or by light cooking. Select couscous that looks fresh and has a fresh aroma and taste. Store in the refrigerator.

DAY 27

BREAKFAST
Veggie patties
Half sweet potatoes
Green tea

LUNCH
Yogurt/mustard chicken fingers
Fruit salad
Applesauce
Bottled water

DINNER
Tuna Paté on top of rice cake
Veggie sticks

HEALTHY CHOICE

TUNA is a great source of zinc and the Omega-3 oils (the "good" fat)—a type of polyunsaturated fat associated with a lower risk of heart disease and possibly other diseases. That's why the American Heart Association recommends eating at least two servings of fish per week. A 3-ounce portion of tuna delivers 21 grams of protein with only 0.7 grams of fat. Its firm, light-colored flesh is the only type of tuna that can be labeled as "white meat" on cans. Its flavor is mild compared to other types of tuna. Whether you like canned tuna or not, you might want to try fresh tuna fillets or steaks. Most people say fresh tuna tastes completely different than canned. It can be grilled, broiled, baked, or poached.

DAY 28

BREAKFAST
Salmon patties
Fruit salad
1/2 cup vanilla yogurt

LUNCH
Black beans/yellow rice
Salad
Carrot sticks
Dill pickles
Red Zinger tea

DINNER
Canned veggie chili
Salad

HEALTHY CHOICE

YOGURT, or fermented milk, isn't mentioned in the Bible, but according to history we know that it was a mainstay at that time. Yogurt has been attributed to longevity in many civilizations. It is the ideal diet food for folks who want to add flavor and health benefits to their diet. Be sure to get the yogurt with "live" bacterial cultures (*Lactobacillus acidophilus*) and without artificial sweeteners or with added sugars. Yogurt is a natural antibiotic that keeps your digestive system healthy by replacing the good flora in the intestinal track. This is needed for a healthy immune system. You can use yogurt in a variety of ways with salad dressings. It's a healthy snack—my favorite is my *Creation's Bounty* Shake with yogurt in the mornings! Those who are lactose-intolerant typically do fine with a good yogurt.

DAY 29

BREAKFAST
Granola bars
Reese's Cup smoothie—organic banana, honey, carob powder, almond butter, Creation's Bounty, yogurt, and organic milk
1 Granny Smith apple

LUNCH
Grilled chicken salad
Rice crackers
Apple wedges with almond butter
Lemonade

DINNER
Yogurt basted chicken breast
Brown rice
Red beans
Salad

HEALTHY CHOICE

BROWN RICE is not as high in protein as wheat and some other grains, but the protein is very good quality and easily usable. Brown rice has its bran layers intact, and therefore all its nutrients are present. The bran protects the germ's fragile fatty acids. It is better in thiamine, biotin, niacin, pyridoxine, and  pantothenic and folic acids than it is in riboflavin and vitamin B12. It has no vitamins A or C, but some vitamin E. Rice, if grown in selenium-rich soil, is very rich in selenium, a scarce but important trace mineral. Magnesium, manganese, potassium, zinc, and iron are all found in good amounts. Sodium is low, but phosphorus, copper, and calcium are all available.

DAY 30

BREAKFAST
Celery sticks stuffed with almond butter
10 almonds
1 boiled egg
Green tea

LUNCH
Salmon quesadillas
Salsa
Spinach salad

DINNER
Faux chicken parmesan
Salad

HEALTHY CHOICE

SALMON is a marine and freshwater fish of the Northern Hemisphere that is a rich source of the Omega-3 oils, which are very important to optimal brain function. Put salmon together with carrots, broccoli, and spinach, 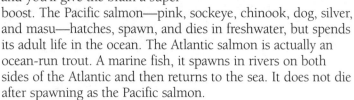 and you'll give the brain a super boost. The Pacific salmon—pink, sockeye, chinook, dog, silver, and masu—hatches, spawn, and dies in freshwater, but spends its adult life in the ocean. The Atlantic salmon is actually an ocean-run trout. A marine fish, it spawns in rivers on both sides of the Atlantic and then returns to the sea. It does not die after spawning as the Pacific salmon.